And It Works

How to create an inexpensive web
site for your business or organization
that gets results.

by

Jack Lehman

CAMBRIDGE, WISCONSIN 2013

BY THE AUTHOR

POETRY
(Under the name John Lehman)

Shrine of the Tooth Fairy
Dogs Dream of Running
Shorts, Brief Poems of
Wonder and Amazement
Acting Lessons
The Village Poet
To the Movies

FICTION

Geography of Sleep
Man with One Ear
Wolves beneath
Chicago
Lit Noir
Men without Meaning
Tales Told in the Dark
Shadows of Unseen Things
Goddess of Unspeakable Things
Lost on Clearview Road
Please Adjust Your Mask
Waiting for Dharma
The Angry Grandfather Chronicles
Not For You Kids
Downward Facing Dog
The All-Night Mystery Story
Sophie Tucker Speaks

NON-FICTION

LEHMAN BIO

He is an advertising and public relations innovator whose Midwest agency did work for Dow Chemical, W.R. Grace and Oscar Mayer as well as for many small businesses. His popular business book is: *Everything Is Changing—How to Gain Loyal Customers and Clients Quickly*.

John (Jack) Lehman is a nationally published writer and poet with twenty years experience as a professional speaker and fifteen years as a creative director and senior copy writer for Midwest advertising agencies. He is a graduate of the Great Books Program at Notre Dame University and has a Masters Degree in Curriculum Development from the University of Michigan. Lehman has presented seminars in several dozen cities throughout the country. He is a book reviewer, business columnist, poet and free-lance feature writer for magazines and newspapers.

His articles have appeared in *The Christian Science Monitor, Popular Science, Omni* and in more than fifty other trade/consumer publications. His plays have been presented in Madison, Milwaukee and in Saint Petersburg, FL. He was awarded the Bronze Star in Vietnam and established "Gear-Up Madison," the largest and oldest non-competitive annual bike ride in Wisconsin.

John lives with his wife, Talia Schorr, and their many dogs and cats in Rockdale, the smallest incorporated village in Wisconsin.

For more information about him, check: www. LehmanInfo.com.

Dedicated to my friend and business cohort for years, Don Hornung.

CONTENTS

Introduction

EVERY "NO" LEADS TO A "YES"

If you are a large advertising specialty company and want to post a catalog of hundreds of promotional products (t-shirts, caps, coffee mugs, etc.) in different colors and sizes that people can order from you, you should hire a web site expert. This is not the book for you.

On the other hand that expert will try to sell a small company or organization much more than they need because that has worked for the expert's big clients who have needed these services...and that is how this person makes money.

The problem, very simply, is not a technical one but a marketing one. Most small businesses don't want to confront questions about what makes them different from their competitors or what real difference any of their products or services provide for the prospect. "Build it and they will come." Right? Hardly. In this age of clutter, success is standing out from everything else bombarding an audience. In showing him or her how you can make that person's life better.

We are not in education or entertainment, but to get someone to do something.

A little goes a long way if people understand how what you offer does this. And you need to connect with them to discover this and then tell others. I'll show you how to : 1. Shape your message; and 2. Utilize web site options that can communicate it inexpensively. But you have to do them. And you should. Even if you hire a consultant, you are the one who knows why your service or product is important to others—the consultant doesn't.

You're the one with something to learn, that will make a difference to your bottom line. It has always been this way, and it is true for a web site also. And finally, this is only one part of the prospect's decision making process. You have to make sure the other steps compliment it. We go from A to B to C to D, not from A to Z.

Your time to start is now. But remember your business or organization is important to us— even if you may experience some stumbles seeing it at first. We need what you do and are cheering for you to succeed.

Chapter 1

WHAT DO YOU WANT?

I worked with a company called "National Promotions" for fifteen or so years. Don had chosen that name because he wanted to impress others that he was more that a Madison, Wisconsin company. It also made him sound good to his family and others who knew him. He was "President of National Promotions."

But what did that mean to prospects? He sold sweatshirts with logos on them, not national exposure. I finally convinced him to change the name to "High Impact." Now if someone was looking through a phone book for promotional items, there was the promise that they would get the ones that were noticeable, memorable.

Still the name was a little vague, and after I left he changed it to "High Impact Branding." "Branding" was a buzz word with advertising agencies a few years ago. Now it seemed a little dated, but actually it spoke to business owners who were a bit behind the times anyway and it sounded right.

I tell my writing workshop students that you have three opportunities with a book cover (and 80% of sales are based on book covers). They are the title. The tag line (the sentence or phrase that runs beneath the title), and the cover image.

Either the title or the tagline must show the benefit to the person of reading (buying) the book and the best picture shows people reaping the rewards for doing this.

My title "And It Works…" promises information that not only will enlighten the reader but get him or her what they want. But that could be about air conditioner repairs or building a space ship, so the tag clarifies this by saying: "How to create an inexpensive web site for your business or organization that gets real results."

I found a picture of someone succeeding with a web site. On the back I put my head shot. I hoped that it would look like a helpful, friendly face of someone who wanted to help but was old enough to have experience doing this.

You may be stuck with a business or organizational name you don't want to change right now. That's fine. It can be small along the top of your site's home page, but you need to come up with a memorable tag line, right now.

It should be from the standpoint of what the customer gets, not what you provide. Take a few minutes and think of two or three tag line possibilities you can try out on friends, family and associates.

Tag Line #1:

Tag Line #2:

Tag Line #3:

When I had my own ad agency our tag line was created when a prospect asked me, "I know how you are different from other agencies in the area, but how are you different from those is Milwaukee, Minneapolis or Chicago. What I came up with was: "No other agency will ever know you so well." It worked because potential customers felt that if people really knew how hard they worked, they would choose to use them. Let's face it, we all feel a little under appreciated. But this tag line was even more important for another reason.

It was something that we, as an agency, had to live up to. If it was a question of doing work we couldn't charge for, but was necessary to make sure it fit what the client needed, by definition we knew we had to go ahead.

For Excel Inns we used the tag line: "The sign of a good night's sleep." I could picture a tired driver going down the highway seeing their motel sign and, bingo, an emotional reaction was almost guaranteed.

Once you have some tag lines, write them out on 3 x 5 cards and pass them out at a business breakfast or after-work gathering. Don't try to lobby for one or the other, listen to what others have to say. You might have to edit the top choice down a bit, but what you have is gold, whether that is on your web site, in an ad or on a coffee cup you give to customers. And try it out on customers and prospects before you get locked into anything. Listen. Listen to what they say and those are the words you can use to convince other prospects.

I have always felt that what customers and people joining organizations want is someone or something that thinks like they do yet has some expertise they don't have but need.

Chapter 2

WHO WILL BUY IT?

Let's say you walk into a crowded room. At a glance who do you think would buy what you have to offer? If you own a jewelry shop, that might be women (but probably those having disposable income, so middle-aged women). If you do retrofit exterior insulation, it might be men who own office buildings or construction contractors.

Even if you are selling all things to all people, you need to decide who are the most profitable customers for you to spend your time and money reaching. But that raises another important question: What are your major sales goals? Take a moment and jot down answers. Perhaps these include "building new business" or "getting different types of business from existing customers." You need to determine what you want, so you can later discover whether or not you have achieved this.

FOUR MAJOR SALES GOALS

1.

2.

3.

4.

If you are having difficulty putting your finger on these, you might want to consider these:

1. Who are your top 10 existing clients (by volume)?

2. How can you get more of their existing business?

3. What is the ideal type of prospect?

4. List some names and phone numbers of names to target.

5. What would make a difference for those you have listed in 4 above—for getting their business

or even for getting an appointment?

6. List your competitors.

7. Name your former customers.

8. Are there some out of town opportunities (we'll talk about resources later, but for now do a little pie-in-the-sky visioning).

This chapter was designed to help you focus. You can check media in your area for demographic matches or with these answers confront a media rep on how they would help you with some kind of action plan. As far as your web site goes. This sets priorities and will help you with tag words to snag search engines. The most important thing for now is that you are consciously trying to decide what sets you apart from your competition and who would be most interested in buying your services. That is where your time and effort should go.

Chapter 3

GETTING RESULTS

Stop!

You probably are thinking, what does any of this have to do with building a website.

It has everything to do with it. The best thing about sales is that your potential customers tell you what they want. The next best thing is that it forces you to think like them. Answer questions before they're asked. Perhaps you don't have a sales person but must do this along with everything else. Believe me this is a gift that will form the products or services you offer in a way that gets results.

So far we have dealt with positioning (what makes you different from your competitors in the eyes of potential customers) and profiling who your best immediate prospects. There are other, subtle things, that we will get into when discussing how to implement these things on the website. But before that, there is one other topic I need to address. It is the most important. The one in which most websites fail. The reason you are creating a site, a business, your life. You need to "ask for the order."

Of course this depends upon your immediate goals. If one is to establish new customers, the order might be for them "to ask for your brochure." The viewer pays for it with his or her name, address, and possibly, e-mail. If it is to get a one-on-one meeting, perhaps you offer a 15% discount that can be redeemed at that time.

Whatever the incentive, the whole web site needs to be designed to lead to this punch line. Remember customers go from A to B to C, not from A to Z, so don't overreach. The purpose is to establish rapport. To ask for the opportunity to get to know one another.

Most of us are afraid of this step because we might fail. And we will, some of the time, but we learn from these experiences so we can succeed even more.

What I have learned is that I need to put my cards on the table and then...shut up.

And then not accept "no." Perhaps, the prospect is shopping around. Let that potential customer make mistakes, but be there for the rebound. Perhaps he or she is going out of business but there is a spark of hope for something new (that's why they are viewing your website). Be there for them. Be part of their rebirth. Better yet, get customer quotation blurbs that show how you have helped accomplish this "rebirth" for others.

Spend a few minutes looking up your competitors on the web. Impressive sites put together by design geeks. They may be eye catching but often they give away too much. Let your viewers want more. How do they get it? That's when you tell them what they have to do next. That's when you "ask for the order."

And what you have to do next is look at the following chapter that focuses on resources, procedures and time lines.

I'll wait here until you do.

Chapter 4

FEATURES VS BENEFITS

A few more questions. Here I am making a distinction between Features and Benefits. Features are things you offer that are special. Years of experience, special skills you or your staff have, etc. These may or may not be important to your potential customer but jot them down.

FEATURES

1.

2.

3.

4.

5.

The next category is called Benefits. In a way you can identify these by asking from the perspective of the prospect, "so what" to the features above. "What do these mean to me. You've been in this business for fifteen years, big deal for you, but why should that matter to me. Oh, you've solved every imaginable problem. I see. So you will know what I need without a lot of background time."

List Benefits. These are what you will use as key points in your copy, as search engine words, in your person-to-person phone call follow up. Once you have these, a great idea is to have existing customers voice them (How do you do that? Simple, ask them to. If they know what you want most people, especially happy customers, will be willing to help.).

BENEFITS

1.

2.

3.

4.

5.

You also need to address the topic of Urgency. Let's face it, even if we need to do something we need a little push to do it now. If you don't want prospects who should act, to procrastinate longer, to shop and shop and shop without ever acting, you have to give them an incentive (or threat) to do it *now*. Perhaps this is a discount offer with a deadline date or a seasonal sale. Let's face it. A web site needs to be active or someone will visit it once or twice and then figure there won't be anything new. Maybe they bookmark you, or maybe they just skim it twice and don't see a need to ever go back.

While we're at it, you should also have a simple, unique image of yourself, your business and a satisfied customer, that are memorable for your viewer. Think of positive impressions you have of products, maybe from your youth—Ronald McDonald, the Wiener Mobile, the Energizer bunny, Hugh Hefner.

When you have a working name, tag line, know who the audience is you want to reach, a list of benefits they can receive, some urgency and a memorable business image, you are ready to go. Well almost ready. There are just a few other points worth considering before you put all this together. We'll address those in the next chapter.

Chapter 5

THE PLAN

Believe it or not, there are still some things you need to address before getting down to the business of making your web site. This is more of an Estimate of Your Situation, and not a bad thing to do, web site or no web site.

ESTIMATE OF YOUR SITUATION

1. First of all, who is doing sales now?

2. How are they compensated for bring business in?

3. What has worked, what hasn't?

4. What sources do you have for referrals (such as a local Chambers of Commerce web site)?

5. How many phone and/or direct contacts do you do per week?

6. What existing computer equipment and programs do you have?

7. Identify the steps usually involved in getting a new client.

8. What are some trouble spots with regard to 7, from their end?

9. What are some trouble spots with regard to 7, from your end?

10. Who are five to ten prospects that should get immediate attention?

11. What existing materials do you have on your products or services (brochures, direct mailers, ads)?

12. What kind of successful offers have you made in the past and what was the immediate result?

13. What long term results are needed:

Public Relations

Advertising

Direct Mail/Phone

Presentations to Clients and Prospects

14. What kind of work area do you have for sales and sales related activities?

15. How much time per day can someone devote to new business?

16. What kind of clerical support is there for a sales effort?

17. Do you have lists of customers and prospects?

18. How efficient is your billing system?

And finally:

19. What can be accomplished in 2 weeks?

20. What can be accomplished in 1 month?

21. What can be accomplished in 3 months?

22. What will need more than 3 months?

Chapter 6

STARTING THE PROCESS

OK, ready? Go to www.1and1.com and check the domain name. Checking is free. There are other host engines (Go Daddy, Network Solutions, Web.Com, iPage, etc.) that will do the same thing, but this is one I have worked with for the past five years so can vouch for it. Whichever you choose the process will be similar. Registering a domain on 1and 1 is as low as $9.99 per year. That could, and should, be the cost of your web site. Total.

You want to start by checking the availability of names under the ".com," ".org" if you are an organization and ".info" when all else fails, which suggests the visitor will be able to get facts he or she needs to make a decision. There are many other choices which the hosting site will try to entice you to buy, by price or availability, but these are the ones with credibility. They say you are established. You know what you are doing. You can be trusted.

Now, I think there are two kinds of domain names. Both are acceptable (and the second type may prove even more memorable). The first is your business name or product or service, such as "RosebudBookReviews.com," that happens to be the name of one of my enterprises.

The second type is usually generated because the first isn't available. It focuses on one of your features or benefits (and may prove a bit longer, so keep this simple). For example a client of mine was Zander Construction. The variations on the name with a ".com" were all taken so I opted for "eifsmaintenance.com." Those of you who don't know "EIFS," in the trade, stands for "exterior insulation finish system." Since Zander was only interested in contractors who were familiar with this and the primary services they offered were maintaining and servicing such installations, it didn't prove a bad choice. Many construction contractors are not that computer savvy, but putting this on the bottom of a trade ad or business card says that Zander is up-to-date. I used "DamnGoodBooks.com" for Zelda Wilde Publishing, even though the ".com" was available, in order to immediately distinguish it from other small publishers.

Be careful. You do *not* need to book all the domain possibilities (".net, .biz, .us, .co," etc.) and make sure that your price for the second, third, fourth years is not out of line with the first year (in other words, watch out for "bait and switch" once they have your credit card number). And, if you do end up, for some reason, getting more domain names, make sure they are all packaged under one price umbrella.

A passage from one of my favorite books, *Zen and the Art of Motorcycle Maintenance*, says it best. The narrator, himself, is a technical writer and a friend wants his reaction to some directions for a rotisserie made in the orient.

"What I wanted to say is that I've a set of instructions at home which begin, 'Assembly of Japanese bicycle require great peace of mind.'"

"Peace of mind isn't at all superficial, really," I expound. "It's the whole thing. That which produces it is good maintenance; that which disturbs it is poor maintenance... If you don't have that when you start and maintain it while you're working you're likely to build your personal problems into the machine itself."

As you set up your web page you will discover there is no one answer. Be open. The craftsman isn't ever following a single line of instruction. He or she is making decisions as they go along. The material and his or her thoughts are changing together in a progression of changes, until his or her mind is at rest at the same time the web site is right.

Sounds more like art than science. It is.

Chapter 7

FINISHING UP

The same thing is true of blog sites that is of domain hosters, except they are FREE. You have you choice of a dozen or so that each have 40 or 50 design choices. Pick one, choose a template, fill in your information, direct your domain URL to it, and you are done.

Except, since these are free they have to make their money some way so they offer all kinds of services you don't need that they do charge for. Be careful of these hooks. Reconcile yourself to learning this for yourself and not settling for anything less than you want. I will walk you through the steps with the service I use, WordPress. But as I have said in prior chapters, the technology (look) is one thing, but to get results you have to know what makes you different, how that benefits potential viewers and, most important, you have to ask for what you want (e-mails, future contact, someone to send a brochure to).

Remember you only have a half minute of viewer

attention to do all this so having a site with a good URL, and designed (at some point) by someone who has a feeling for layout, graphics and typography make a difference. That is what the blog sites, such as those of WordPress, offer.

Now go to www.wordpress.com. Select "Create a New Blog." Next place your blog name in the address space (this will come up with the ".wordpress.com" after it. Don't worry, I'll show you how to sidestep this if you already have a domain name and host).

You'll see that several of the ones you may have had in mind are taken. No problem, just get something that works. You will direct the web host URL to the blog page and none of that other will show up in the address at the top of the page any way.

Enter your blog name.

Finally go down to the bottom of the page and click "Sign Up" in the column designated "Free Blog Site." You are ready to begin choosing a template and substituting your own text.

On your "Dashboard" go down the column of features to one identified as "Appearance." First item when you do will be "Available Themes."

Begin work on the actual site by choosing and previewing templates. Some are free, some cost extra. I think the free ones are as good as the premium ones. Anyway start with these. Now the template you choose is one that best fits the content you want to empathize. You can change these at any time, so have some fun with this. Your name will appear on the previewed template. Later you will change other wording.

Once you have made your choice, go back to the design (under "Appearances"), now at the top of your computer screen. There are two additional choices. The first is "Custom." When you click this you will have alternate choices for: Headings, Tag Lines, Colors (type and background), Downloadable Images, Fonts and, if you want, the viewer to first encounter either a Front Page or Recent Posts (Choose Front Page).

Your last task is to Customize Widgets (these are the items, usually to the left or right on the page that offer links, books for sale, listings of posts).

That's plenty for this chapter. Go ahead and give it a try. Don't get discouraged. This is exploration. The right fit is out there, finding it means keeping options open.

Chapter 8

STEP BY STEP

I am going to take a web site that I have been thinking about doing and walk you through each of the steps using it as an example. Mine deals with writing, but don't worry about that. The example should work for what you need too.

1. I choose some possible URL designations. Mine are: a) "WritePoemsAndShort Stories.com," b) "WritePoemsAndShort Stories.info" and c) "WriteWhatYouWouldLoveToRead.com."
2. I go to 1and1.com.
3. I test the first (it is shorter and less complicated than my other choice). It is available.
4. I buy that domain name, entering my credit card information.
5. I go to wordpress.com and click on "Create a New Blog"
6. I enter my domain name to the address and the blog name, "Write Poems And Short Stories." The latter, I space out.

They add ".wordpress.com" to the address.

7. Going to the bottom of the page, I click "Free Blog Site."

8. Still at <u>wordpress.com</u>, on my Dashboard, I go to appearance and click on "Themes."

9. I now choose a theme template. My choice is "Sunspot." I don't know about the white type on the black background. If there is a lot of copy it will prove difficult to read. I decide not to have a lot of copy.

10. My Blog name appears on the template, but I need to put a "Tag Line" under it. I go to customize on the "Theme Page" and click "Customize." My tag line is the name of my book "The Art of Dancing in the Rain." I could have used, "Write What You'd Love to Read" but chose the other as being a little more imaginative since the blog name is so direct.

11. One other thing, as long as I am at it, is to designate a static first page as opposed to one having my latest "Posts." That way I can get the most basic information across, then direct

viewers to pages that speak to their particular interest.

12. My next stop, under "Appearance" is "Widgets." I eliminate all that are on the initial design except: "Contact" which has my name, telephone number, and e-mail; "Image" where I put an enticing drawing of a perspective viewer; "Text." Here I will put the covers and links to buying my books, either to CC Now or to Amazon; and finally "Links" where I put my other web sites and perhaps one or two of friends who are doing the same for me.

13. One that you may not want (a promo for WordPress) that seems hard to eliminate is "Blogroll." Simply go into "Links" on your Dashboard and get rid of all the listings.

14. One note, when you want a picture you click "Media" on the Dashboard (above the section where you are putting text). Download pictures from your picture files, or from http://commons.wikimedia.org (these are in the public domain if you give Wikimedia credit). When they are in

your media library, if you click on the title of each it provides a URL that can be used in your "Image" Widget.

15. Let me end with a distinction that may prove important. A "Post" is an individual entry on the same page as other "Posts." It is handy if you are an organization and have weekly messages, such as events, for your viewers. Most businesses use "Pages" which are more or less static. Each tells of a service or product the viewer can find out more about (but please have a "Call to Action" at the end of each).

CHAPTER 9

MORE POSSIBILITIES

There are two things specifically you might want to consider to make money. These belong at the top of your Widgets. The first is a phone number where prospects can reach you directly. Many web sites put this on a Contact page. Personally, I feel if you have to look for it, the business or organization doesn't really want you to contact them. I like a bold phone number and e-mail address (you can get a connection to your personal e-mail through a name, such as "john@DamnGoodBooks.com"from the domain site (URL) that is then redirected to your regular e-mail).

The other possibility is to offer something for a price, a book or packet of material, for example. For this you will need to have a vehicle that accepts credit cards. I recommend CC Now, even though Pay Pal is the other well-known service. Both charge a small monthly fee. I have CC Now and after a year of a minimal monthly charge, they dropped it (that happened several years ago and they have not bothered me for it since, though their service is still going).

What you need, for both Widget and credit card service is an image of what you are offering and brief description. The nice thing about this is that it provides immediate income. And though that may not be much, I feel someone who makes a small money decision is more likely to commit to some larger amount at a later time.

Years ago I did the marketing for a new home construction process using foam walls. We sold information packets for $10 each and made more that way than ever building homes.

What's important to *you* when *you* make a buying decision? Take a few minutes and think about a purchase you may have made during the last six months or so — something substantial that wasn't an impulse buy. Examples might be deciding on a new car, a television or where to take an extended vacation.

What were your pre-purchase thoughts? Recall your expectations and the considerations that went into your decision-making process. Was there a specific need you were meeting, any desire to prove something by making this purchase or were you solving some immediate problem? (Actually stop reading for a minute and give this some thought.)

When you help someone make a wise buying decision, you form a working partnership that is the sound basis of future business.

Chapter 10

THE BIGGER PICTURE

Now try to identify the stages you went through in that buying process. Did you check the newspaper, ask a friend about his or her experience, visit several stores? Did you compare features? What role did a salesperson play?

Next, try to analyze your reasons for the specific purchase. Compare your pre-purchase expectations (your original mental picture of having this product) with the attributes of the product or service you actually selected. How do you feel now, after having made the purchase and having used the product or service for awhile? Think about *utility* (how well it works), *value* (was it worth the price you paid?) and *satisfaction* (how happy are you with the purchase?).

Typically in the purchasing process, 85% of our time is spent in clarifying our needs and in solving problems as to how those needs will be met. Only 10% of our effort is concerned with product features and benefits, and less than 5% is concerned with making the actual purchase. If you're helping someone with a buying decision, shouldn't your effort in each of these areas proportionately match those percentages?

Move from *need* to *desire* to *trust* to *action*. The left channel on my stereo goes out, for example. I have a need to get the system fixed or replace it. I start noticing ads in magazines and newspapers about some new features that would make my listening to music even more enjoyable. Perhaps there's a certain brand name that catches my fancy and I ask a neighbor, or a co-worker whose opinion I trust, what he or she thinks of that make. I go to the store with several options in mind and ask the sales clerk, who I don't know, what I should do.

NEED	DESIRE	TRUST	ACTION

→

Broken Stereo	Comparing Features	Brand Recognition	Purchase
Marketing	Advertising	Public Relations	Sales

Each of these stages has its own parallel in the world of mass communications and mass merchandising. Marketing identifies *need*, advertising sparks *desire*, public relations builds *trust,* and sales is the call to *action*. The first letter of each of these—Marketing, Advertising, Public Relations and Sales—spells out MAPS.

In reviewing my example of the stereo, I had a definite need because the system I was using just wasn't working anymore. When I decided to buy a new stereo, I became aware of features, such as changers that would play six hours of CD's. I could envision enjoying this feature; programming the music for an evening when having people over for dinner. I started to notice features like this in newspaper ads, but I was also aware from these ads that, since I had purchased my last system, there were many new brands I hadn't heard of before. Asking someone more knowledgeable than myself about sound systems gave me ideas of three or four manufactures that I might trust. When I go to the store and find more or less what I want I ask the clerk if I should buy now or wait for a possible sale. He tells me what he would do, and I follow his advice.

I am making my way along the "decision making path." Each transaction has various stages. In fact, they are like the arrow signs tacked on trees to lead you through a path in the woods. They don't necessarily go in a straight line, but what is important to you is to get from one arrow to the next. If you do that successfully, you'll get to your destination.

Your task is to discover what each of these segments or stages is for your potential customer and then to determine what that person needs in order for the transaction to proceed to the next stage.

In reality, this is seldom a linear process, though for the sake of analysis, let's treat it as if it were. It's unlikely that someone's feeling satisfied at only one stage will jump to a final decision. A common mistake, for example, is to assume that because your product has the lowest price, a person buying it doesn't also need to have *need*, *desire, trust* and *vision* before he or she will commit. Price is only one aspect of *need*.

Chapter 11

THE PROCESS CONTINUED

Always keep the buyer's perspective in mind throughout these stages. To achieve a profitable sale and a satisfied loyal customer, you need to understand the selling process from the purchaser's point of view — from the earliest awareness through user satisfaction after the product or service has been used. Trying to get someone to buy a product or a services without understanding these stages is following a dated view of selling as "product-pushing" (though "product pushing" is tempting because it's more comfortable for salespeople to *tell* rather than *ask*, to *talk* rather than *listen*). But by ignoring or working *against* the customer's decision making process, you cause confusion, resentment, wasted time and lost sales.

What is energizing about thinking of this process in stages is that it forces you, the business person, to act in terms of the here and now at each of these benchmarks. The objective is to get to the next stage, but not by trying to follow a formula which may have worked for you in the past. In a way, this seems like we are giving up control. It would be nice to think there is a sure-fire script that always leads to "yes" or a clever set of answers that satisfy every prospect's objections. In reality, these are illusions. You are not giving up control, just the illusion of having something that never existed. Instead, you now have to get a better grasp on what's really happening.

Isn't it failed expectations based on our attachment to things that have worked in other circumstances that lead to our feeling frustrated and discouraged? Give up these expectations! They are limiting and represent a mindless approach. Being fully aware means taking every moment for what it is. Not only is this freeing, it is also more fun.

Remember: Every time one of our customers or prospects makes a buying decision, he or she does so through a sequence of stages or steps. The steps of the decision-making process provide you opportunities to act.

By responding at each stage with your full awareness, you discover either:

a. A solid fit between this person's needs and the product or service you're recommending which will lead to a sale; or

b. There is not a fit, and you shouldn't be doing business together (which is valuable information for focusing your time and effort). Through the buying process you always end up with more than the individual sales call or sale.

Chapter 12

FOCUS, CLARIFY, SUPPORT, VISUALIZE

There are 4-things you can do to hone your message and create tools that will turn your customers into advocates. These are: *Focus, Clarify, Support* and *Visualize*.

Focus means to zero in on your target audience with the information it needs to hear at this stage of the buying process. To do that, go back to Chapter 2. Who should this be directed at? What obstacle is this person facing and what have you identified as a way of overcoming this obstacle? These become the opening lines of your web site.

Sometimes this takes the form of a statement, a promise or a question, such as, "A woman wants more from her doctor than a man does." It is followed closely with information that clarifies and develops the opening idea—detailing what this means in real terms for the person receiving the message. You're now emphasizing the business and personal benefits of the "solution" you are offering. For example, our opening statement, "A woman wants more from her doctor than a man does." might be immediately clarified by, "You want private, reassuring, personalized health care that spans your life. A commitment to preventative care and the specialized training to handle the not-so-routine. You want a doctor who does more than just help you stay well...you want a doctor who treats you well."

Next your message must support your claim and clarifying remarks. Use storytelling techniques to involve your audience and convince them of the truth of what you're saying. Quotes, testimonials and hypothetical situations make the content come alive and give it credibility. On a web site stating, "Our publications deliver tangible results" a clarifying paragraph states: "To be successful your newsletter or magazine must accomplish three objectives: 1) It must simplify your readers' lives, giving them information they want and truly value. 2) It must facilitate your operational efficiency, and 3) It must dramatize your uniqueness in areas where you face your toughest competition." One of several testimonials says, "Our Credit Union members consistently rate *GoodTimes* magazine, produced by Grey Publishing, as their most valuable membership benefit. Readers like how it informs and entertains. We know it helps our organization retain members and attract new ones."

And finally, you want your audience to apply what you're saying to their own situation, to visualize success using the product or services you are offering. Inherent in this step is the action that will bring this about. You must always tell the person receiving your message the results they can expect, the process that will lead to these results and the next step they have to take if this is something they want. "Contact us without delay. Grey Publishing knows the elements that guarantee publishing success. Let us meet briefly to discuss your specific needs in terms of what your readers want and determine how a publication can enhance their lives and your organization's effectiveness. At a follow-up presentation we will show you how to achieve these results and communicate the unique advantages you offer. We'll also give you a realistic timeline for accomplishing this. There is no cost or obligation. Call us at 608-257-4740."

The secondary objective of every marketing, advertising public relations and sales tool is to help customers overcome a reluctance to change. That reluctance is there even if change is to their advantage. So present an alternative reality in which the prospect is using your product or service instead of what he or she is now buying? The answer is that you must create "a picture" that seems almost as tangible as the real situation.

Focus, Clarify, Support and *Visualize* are the main objectives. If creating an alternative reality to help customers overcome a reluctance to change is a second objective, then a third should be communicating quality—not in words or slogans, but by the materials you use to convey your message. The subliminal message of quality fosters trust. It says to a client, this company cares enough to do it right, they are professionals in this and they will be professionals in the products and services they deliver.

AFTERWARDS

YOUR TURN

You may feel awkward in developing these tools. It's not something you're accustomed to. You wouldn't sit down to a piano if you had never played one before and expect to perform Rachmaninoff. You don't have to be an expert from the start. It's more important that you do start. And like everything else in business, and in life, you will grow in proficiency as you grow in experience. It goes back to the concept of *kaizen*, a small refinement made daily that begins to create compounded results, or constant improvement, at a level beyond what was envisioned. By the time you need to be expert in producing a web site you will have progressed to that level and be able to do it.